INTRODUCTION

For some years already, taking the creation of paper toys as a hobby has been on the rise. Artists from the graphic design world, comic artists, illustrators, graffiti artists... all contribute to this phenomenon. International designers and graphic artists create impressive templates to share them later, in a totally altruistic manner, on their websites and blogs, so their followers can download them and create fantastic paper toys.

The tools are very simple: paper, scissors, glue and some patience to put together these marvellous dolls. The most exciting is to see how, from a paper sheet, we can easily create from the scratch a 3D object with no limit for creative possibilities. The main idea is very simple: Make it yourself!

The book includes 32 templates printed on an excellent quality on 200gr couché paper, which can be used to create 24 fabulous paper toys, designed by artists from all over the world, and have these little pieces of art in your own house!

Desde hace algunos años, ha aumentado la afición por realizar muñecos de papel. Artistas del mundo del diseño gráfico, dibujantes de cómic, ilustradores, grafiteros... contribuyen a este fenómeno, creando impresionantes plantillas que más tarde comparten, de una forma totalmente altruista, para que sus seguidores las puedan descargar y crear fantásticos *paper toys*.

Las herramientas son muy sencillas: papel, tijeras, pegamento y un poco de paciencia para montar estos muñecos maravillosos. Lo más emocionante es ver como de una hoja de papel podemos crear fácilmente, partiendo casi de la nada, un objeto tridimensional sin límite de posibilidades creativas. La idea principal es muy simple: ¡Hazlo tú mismo!

El libro incluye 32 plantillas impresas con una excelente calidad en papel couché de 200gr, con los que poder crear 24 fabulosos *paper toys*, diseñados por artistas de todo el mundo, ¡y tener en tu propia casa estas pequeñas obras de arte!

Capkids. Deerest Friends edition.

PAUL SHIH

www.paul-shih.com
www.hollowthreat.com
NEW ZEALAND

"I love paper toys! I believe it has always been my calling. I've been collecting collected toys since I was a kid, and never stopped hunting for cool new toys; one of my dreams was to see my characters in 3-D form some day. As an artist, I think we all try hard to live our own dreams, so I'm constantly looking for ways to make toys. Obviously, the easiest way and the most accessible medium is paper! My first paper toy was Big-Foot, back in 2006, and the design was created as an aid for a paper diorama I did back then; it also served as a small tribute to the mythic creature called Sasquatch. The great thing about paper toys is that they are really easy to obtain; you don't need a credit card or to travel anywhere to buy them. When I uploaded my Big-Foot toy to my Web site, I asked the downloader to participate in my Big-Foot Exists Project; all they had to do was to build the toy and send a photo of the Big-Foot taken in their area, and I've been getting photos from all over the world, "sightings" of Sasquatch! I really enjoy the interaction between paper toys and those who download them. It's something regular toys can never provide; paper toys not only make me feel closer to those who like my creation, they also bring artists together. TNES and I put together the "T-Wrecks" paper toy template in '07. We invited some of our friends and favorite artists to customize it, and the outcome was mindblowing. You never know what you will get. There are just endless possibilities for paper toys."

"¡Me encantan los *paper toys*! Colecciono juguetes y muñecos desde que era un niño. Como artista, creo que todos nos esforzamos por alcanzar nuestros sueños, por eso estoy buscando constantemente mil maneras de crear mis propios muñecos. Obviamente, la manera más fácil y el medio más accesible es el papel. Mi primer *paper toy* fue Big-Foot, en el año 2006, lo diseñé para un diorama de papel que hice en aquel entonces, y que a su vez también fue un pequeño homenaje a la mítica criatura llamada Sasquatch. Lo mejor de los *paper toys* es que son muy fáciles de conseguir, no necesitas una tarjeta de crédito, o viajar a cualquier lugar para comprarlos. Cuando subí mi Big Foot a mi página web, pedí a los internautas que participaran en mi proyecto ¡El Big Foot existe!; todo lo que tenían que hacer era montar el *paper toy* y enviar una foto del Big-Foot tomada en su ciudad. He estado recibiendo fotos de todo el mundo: ¡Avistamientos de Sasquatch!. Me gusta mucho la interacción entre los *paper toys* y los que los descargan. Es algo que los muñecos normales nunca puede proporcionar, los *paper toys* me hacen sentir más cerca de los que le gusta mi arte. El artista TNES y yo hicimos juntos la plantilla "T-Wrecks" en el 2007; invitando a algunos de nuestros amigos y artistas favoritos para que lo personalizaran, y la respuesta fue una locura, nunca sabes qué va a pasar, las posibilidades con los *paper toys* son infinitas".

T-Wrecks. Rainbow Kaiju Edition.
Template by Grooph and customized by Paul Shih.

T-Wrecks.
Template by TNES and Paul Shih. Customized by Paul Shih.

Big-Foot.

Totem Hollow Threat.
Template by Dolly Oblong and customized by Paul Shih.

MACULA

Christopher Bonnette
www.macula.tv/papercraft
www.flickr.com/photos/macula1
CALIFORNIA (USA)

"I love paper toys because they are fun to build and can be share with people all around the world. With only a few craft supplies and a little time, you can have your very own custom toy. It is one of the most inexpensive ways an artist can design their own toy. Paper toys are also like model kits; you have to invest some time into building each one, making it more of a prized possession. It is very nice to see people taking their time to build one of your creations and being so proud they made it themselves."

"Me encantan los *paper toys* porque es muy divertido construirlos y compartirlos con personas de todo el mundo. Con pocos medios y con un poco de tiempo, puedes tener tu propio *paper toy*. Es una de las maneras más baratas para que un artista diseñe su propio muñeco. Los *paper toys* son una especie de recortables, hay que invertir tiempo en su construcción, por lo que se convierten en un bien muy preciado. Es muy satisfactorio ver como las personas invierten su tiempo en construir uno de mis *paper toys* y que se sientan tan felices al realizarlos".

Base Folk Paper Toys.

Page 12: **Tiki.**
This page: **La Catrina.**
Chibi Yeti.

All paper toys.

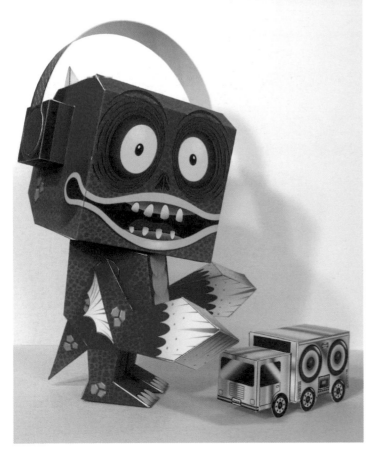

Kaiju.

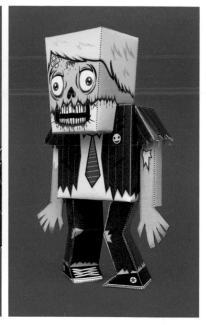

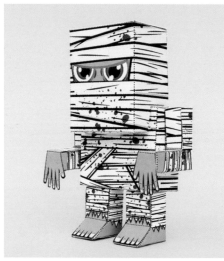
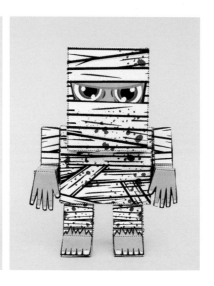

DADIK TRIADI AKA DYADIK

www.dikids.blogspot.com
Jakarta
INDONESIA

"There are many reasons why I really love paper toys: they are cheap, useful, innovative, environmentally friendly, and it's easy to get and build awesome paper toys from all around the world. All you need is an Internet connection, a printer, a pair of scissors, glue, and a little time to build them. I love creating paper toy designs because it is good exercise for both my brain and my sense of creativity. Paper toys have always blown my mind, because when you see a flat piece of paper turn into a three-dimensional object, it feels like magic–from the intangible to the tangible. A paper toy is not just a toy, it is a new canvas on creating great art. That's why I fell in love with paper toys."

"Hay muchas razones por las que me encantan los *paper toys*: son baratos, útiles, innovadores, ecológicos, y son fáciles de obtener y construir, todo lo que necesitas es una conexión a Internet, una impresora, unas tijeras, pegamento y un poco de tiempo para construirlos. Me encanta la creación de *paper toys* ya que es un ejercicio bueno para mi cerebro y mi sentido de la creatividad. Los *paper toys* siempre han volado por mi mente, porque cuando ves como un pedazo de papel se convierte en un objeto tridimensional, se siente la magia de lo intangible a lo tangible. Un *paper toy* no es sólo un juguete, es un nuevo lienzo para crear grandes obras de arte. Por eso me enamoré de los *paper toys*".

Left page, from top to bottom: **Dead worker, Mummy, Woodbiter.**
This page: **Sid and Nancy.**

Rorobotan.

Astro Dumpy.

Bottle Smoker.

Darth Fater.

Ico Bot and Zurg.

DOLLY OBLONG

www.dollyoblong.com
THE NETHERLANDS

"I'm a plush maker and paper toy designer who fills every spare minute knitting cute, cuddly creatures, building pieces of Paper Totem, doodling, designing, and keeping track of all things happening in my world on my blog. I love collecting toys, I'm mad about bunnies, and do not start a day without a cup of Earl Grey! Last but not least, I love collaborating with other artists from around the world. What I like most about paper toys is that anybody with basic materials like a printer, scissors, and some glue can start their own toy collection! As a designer, it's easy to connect with a worldwide audience, because most paper toys are freely available for download. For me, paper toys are about pushing myself creatively and getting designs out there."

"Soy una diseñadora de muñecos de peluche y *paper toys* que invierte cada minuto de su tiempo tejiendo divertidas criaturas, construyendo figuras para mi proyecto "Paper Totem", dibujando, bocetando y haciendo el seguimiento de todas las cosas que me suceden en mi blog. Me encanta coleccionar muñecos, me vuelven loca los conejos, y no empiezo nunca el día sin tomar una taza de té Earl Grey. Por último pero no menos importante, me gusta colaborar con artistas de todo el mundo. Lo que más me gusta de los *paper toys* es que cualquiera con materiales básicos como una impresora, tijeras y pegamento puede comenzar su propia colección de muñecos. Como diseñadora, es fácil conectar con público de todo el planeta, porque la mayoría de los *paper toys* están disponibles gratuitamente para su descarga".

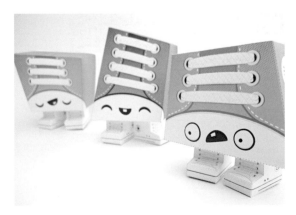

Paper kicks.

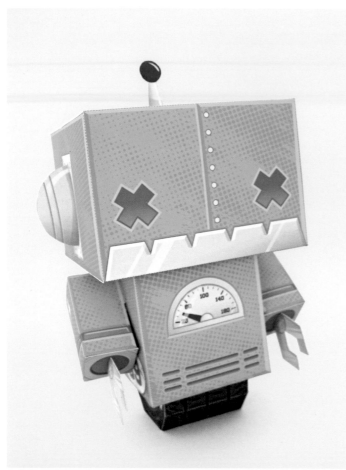

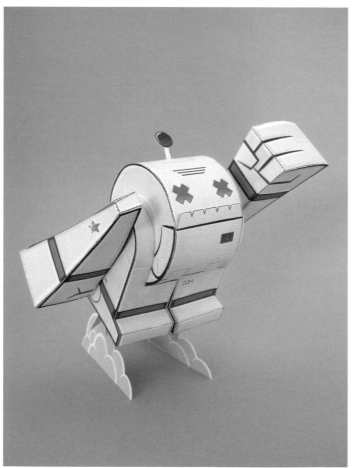

Left page, up: **Dairobo GoGo.** Custom Cubeecraft (model designed by Cubeecraft).

Left page, down: **Dairobo Ryo.** Custom ye-boT (model designed by Marko Zubak).

This page, top: **Jelly.**
Bottom: **Kazu.**

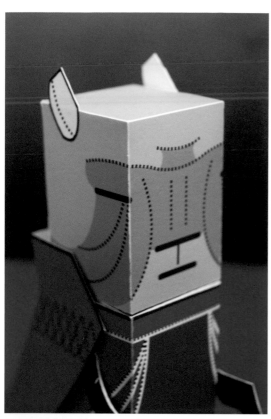

Retro Demon.

HORRORWOOD

Jack Hankins
www.horrorwood.info
JAPAN

"Well, I love toys and I love illustration, and paper toys are a natural fusion of the two. I have always wanted to create three-dimensional objects, ideally my own toys, but my crafting skills are very limited. Therefore, paper craft gave me the means to turn my two-dimensional ideas into real world products with ease. I create most of my illustrations digitally, so shifting to creating templates for paper craft was not so hard. Paper craft is great because it brings together art, design, and craft, so I get to do all these things at once. Some time ago, I designed my first paper toys and made them available for download on my Web site. I started getting very positive feedback, after which I decided to put all of my energy into producing papercraft, and haven't looked back ever since. This is another great thing about working with paper. Thanks to the Internet, you can now easily distribute your artwork to people all around the world. Not only that, but people end up with a physical object in their hands. I can't think of any other medium that works quite like this. Unknowingly, I have found myself in the middle of a real paper boom. A couple of years ago, the papercraft scene began to explode globally, and the community is growing day after day. Everyone collaborates and communicates, and there is a constant flow of activity and new projects. This is a really exciting time to be a paper artist."

"Me encantan los juguetes y la ilustración, y los *paper toys* son una fusión natural de ambas cosas. Siempre he querido crear objetos tridimensionales, especialmente mis propios muñecos. Todas mis ilustraciones las creo digitalmente, por lo que diseñar plantillas para hacer *paper toys* no fue muy difícil para mi. Crear con papel es muy fácil porque reúne arte, diseño y artesanía, todo en uno, y yo puedo hacer todas esas cosas sin ningún problema. Hace algún tiempo, diseñé mis primeros *paper toys* y los colgué en mi página web. Tuve una respuesta muy positiva, por lo que puse todos mis esfuerzos en producir más y más muñecos de papel. Gracias a internet, puedes distribuir tu arte con facilidad y llegar a la gente de cualquier rincón del mundo. Inevitablemente me he visto en medio de un verdadero boom del papel. Hace unos años, la escena de los *paper toys* explotó a nivel global y la comunidad sigue creciendo día a día. Todo el mundo colabora y se comunica, y hay un constante flujo de actividad y nuevos e interesantes proyectos. Es un momento muy excitante para ser un *paper artist*".

Ghosts in the Machine.

Toro Oscuro.

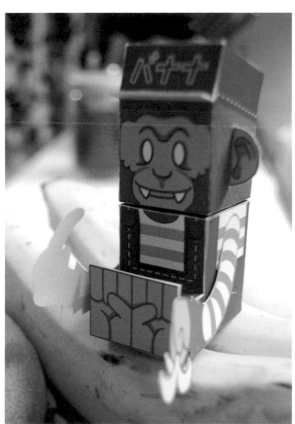

Go Bananas.

The Long Paw of the Law.

Stereobot Sticky Fingers. Design by Ivan Ricci, inspired by famous Hirohiko Araki's Manga "JoJo's Bizarre Adventure".

Stereobot. Design by Ivan Ricci.

IVAN RICCI

www.kawaii-style.net
www.flickr.com/photos/kawaii-style
ITALY

"Paper toys are fantastic. I keep them on my desk and on the shelf above my computer because they inspire me and make me happy. I like to see my graphic works on three-dimensional objects, and I think it's wonderful to be able to share my paper toys with many other people. It's nice to know they have them somewhere in their homes, perhaps very far from here. While it's great that paper toys are free, I would love to create a commercial line using more sophisticated crafting techniques, high-quality paper, and special ink, to make them even more unique and beautiful."

"Los *paper toys* son fantásticos. Me gusta ponerlos en mi escritorio y en la estantería cerca de mi ordenador porque me inspiran y me hacen feliz. Me gusta ver mis gráficos convertidos en objetos tridimensionales, y pienso que es maravilloso poder compartir mis *paper toys* con otra gente. Me gusta saber que hay quienes los tiene en sus casas, quizás muy lejos de aquí. Aunque lo mejor de todo es que los *paper toys* son gratis, me gustaría crear una línea comercial usando técnicas más sofisticadas, papeles de alta calidad, tintas especiales, para hacerlos si es posible aún mucho más únicos y bonitos".

Kawaii Kuma-chan. Based on Calling all Cars template by Horrorwood.
Design and photo by Ivan Ricci.

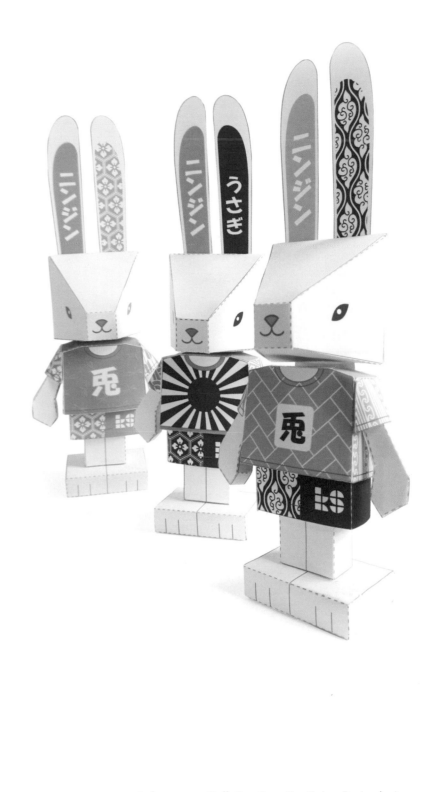

Left page, up: **HelloCoy PaperToy Enjoy.** Design by Ivan Ricci, based on HelloCoy template by Salazad.

Left page, down: **HelloCoy Tokyo Yomiuri Giants.** Design by Ivan Ricci, based on HelloCoy template by Salazad.

This page: **Bunny Boy Japan taste.** Design and photo: Ivan Ricci. Produced: Paper in the Country.

This page, bottom:
Jesus, Joseph, and Maria. Paper toy Christmas cards. Designed for 013 Popcentre.
Woot Bots. Paper toy robots.

LOULOU AND TUMMIE

Laurens Schellekens
www.loulouandtummie.com
THE NETHERLANDS

"We love and collect toys, so the choice to start making our own paper toys came naturally. And, of course, it's very easy and cheap to share them with everyone around the globe! Besides those practical considerations, we also enjoy figuring out ways to fit the template for the toy on a single sheet of paper. There's fun in making the template design look good on its own, as well as coming up with ways of integrating the instructions in the design. The instructions have to be easy to follow and at the same time match the style of the overall design."

"Nos encantan los muñecos y también coleccionarlos, por lo que decidimos empezar a hacer nuestros propios *paper toys* de una forma natural, y por supuesto, es muy fácil y barato compartirlos con todo el mundo. También nos gusta retorcernos el cerebro para ver como diseñamos la plantilla de cada nuevo *paper toy* que creamos en una simple hoja de papel. Es muy divertido diseñar la plantilla para que sea atractiva en sí misma, y también el como integrar las instrucciones de montaje en el diseño final. Las instrucciones tienen que ser fáciles de seguir y a su vez que tengan una coherencia con el diseño global de cada *paper toy*".

Dr. Iso.

Baby Robot.

Small selection of paper toys family.

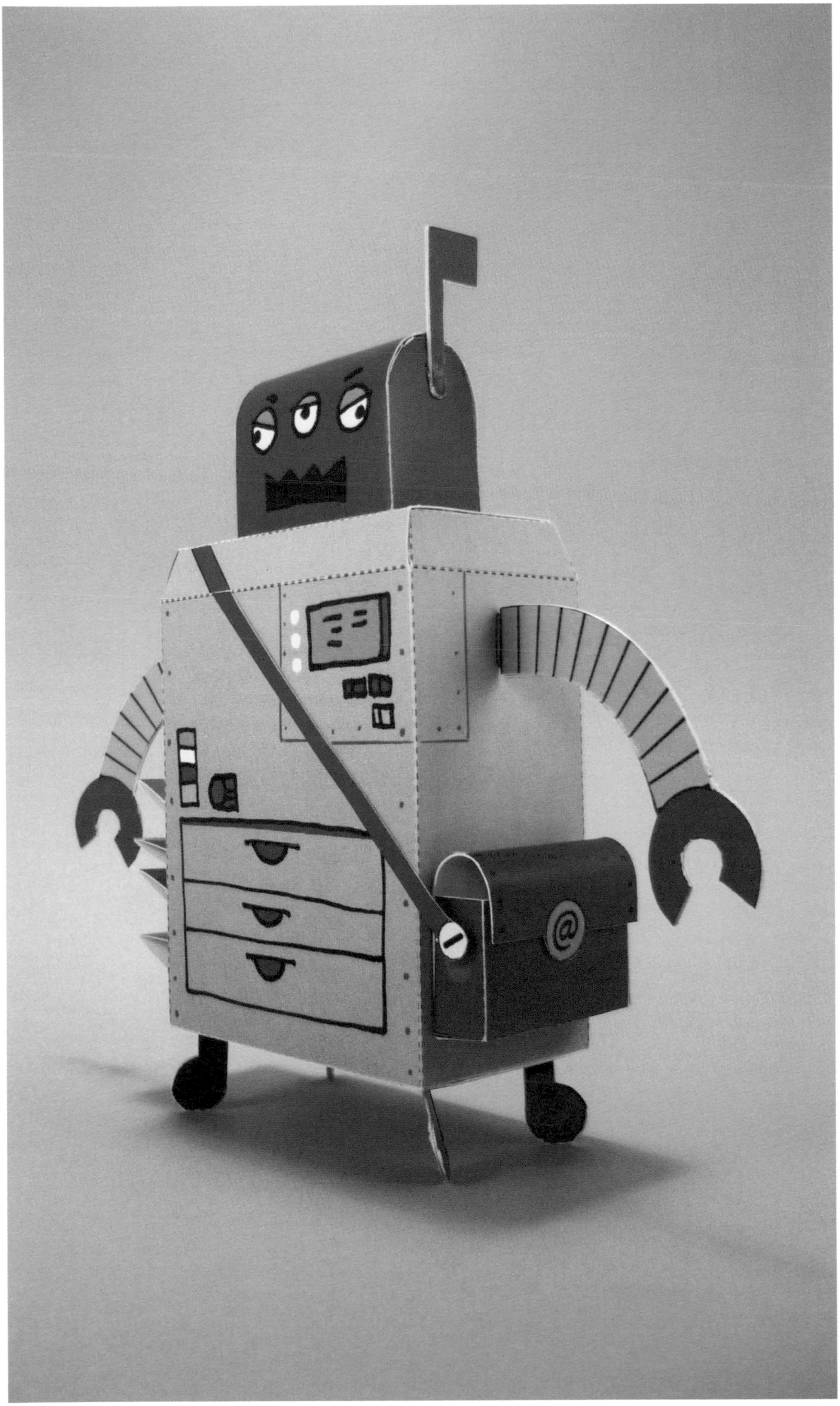

Spambot.
Designed for Fine Design /
Norton Symantec.

SHIN TANAKA

www.shin.co.nr
JAPAN

"I love paper toys because paper is the most beautiful material in the world, with smooth curves and sharp lines. And it is part of daily life. People can download the templates from the Internet and exchange them. Customizing them is also easy; people can make their own paper toys. Creating with paper is much faster than with other materials, such as plastic and vinyl. Paper toys are always fresh!"

"Me encantan los *paper toys* porque el papel es el material más bello del mundo, adoro sus suaves curvas y sus líneas estilizadas, además el papel forma parte de nuestro día a día. Crear con papel es mucho más rápido que con cualquier otro material, como el plástico o el vinilo. La gente puede descargar las plantilas de sus *paper toys* favoritos de internet, intercambiarlas y personalizarlas fácilmente. Los paper toys están siempre frescos!"

Gw.

Br.

Hoophy on a wall.

Hoophy 144%.

TETSUYA WATABE

www.kamimodel.com
JAPAN

"I like the texture of paper. It's easy to shape into anything I want. I think it's attractive for flat surfaces to change into three dimensional objects. And I can make papercraft with simple tools. I designed Rommy so that a beginner in papercraft could build it. If many people build it and feel an affinity for the character, I will feel very happy."

"Me encanta la textura del papel. Es muy fácil darle cualquier forma que me guste. Creo que es muy atractivo covertir superficies totalmente lisas en objetos tridimensionales y las herramientas que se necesitan son muy sencillas.
Diseñé mi *paper toy* "Rommy" de tal manera que cualquier principiante lo pueda montar fácilmente. Me haría muy feliz que todo aquel que lo monte sienta afinidad con el personaje".

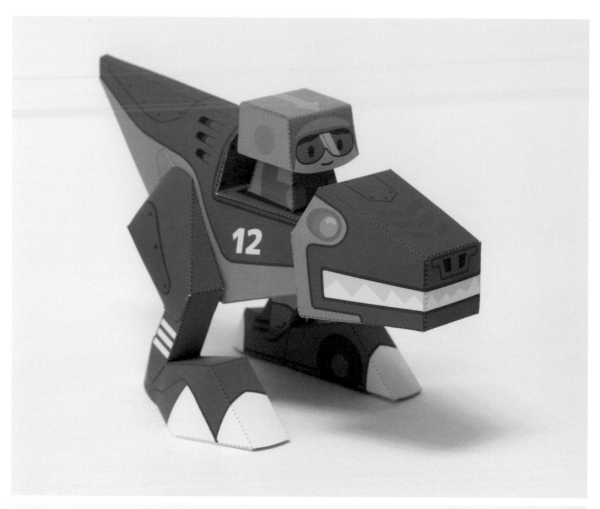

Page 40, from top to bottom:
Quororoy Panda, Giant Anteater and **Rommy.**
Page 41:
Red Dragon.

This pages:
Dinogoo.

From top to bottom:
Sandy Jr and **Sandy.**
Apple Pop and **Marky.**

CUBOTOY

Angello García Bassi
Academic at the School of Design of Diego Portales University
www.cubotoy.cl
CHILE

My name is Angello García Bassi, I am a Graphic Designer and academic at the School of Design of Diego Portales University. Since 2007 I have developed my creative work under the name of "Cubotoy", creating products and collaborating with several brands and institutions, using the paper as experimental material. My designs are the first collectible paper toys developed in Chile, and they are used as educational material in schools and universities. My work has been exhibited at the MAD Museum of Arts and Design in New York, and published in the book "Cubotoy: A World of Paper".

Mi nombre es Angello García Bassi, soy Diseñador Gráfico y académico en la Escuela de Diseño de la Universidad Diego Portales. Desde el año 2007 he desarrollado mi trabajo creativo bajo el nombre "Cubotoy" creando productos y colaboraciones con diversas marcas e instituciones, utilizando el papel como material de experimentación. Mis diseños son los primeros juguetes de papel coleccionables desarrollados en Chile y son utilizados como material educativo en colegios y universidades. Mi trabajo fue expuesto en el MAD Museum of Arts and Design de New York y publicado en el libro "Cubotoy: Un Mundo de Papel".

From top to bottom:
Aku Aku and **Moai.**
Sandy & Louis and his alter ego **Louis Mask.**

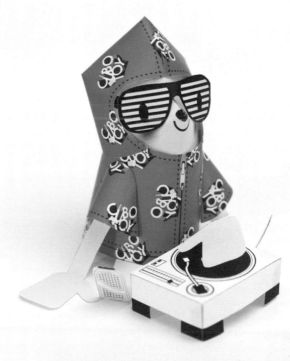

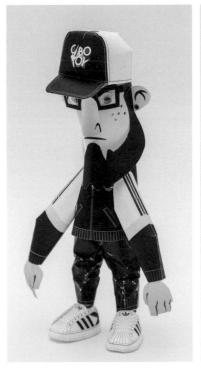

From top to bottom:
Sandy Dj.
Joe and **Louis Mask.**

47

INDEX OF TEMPLATES

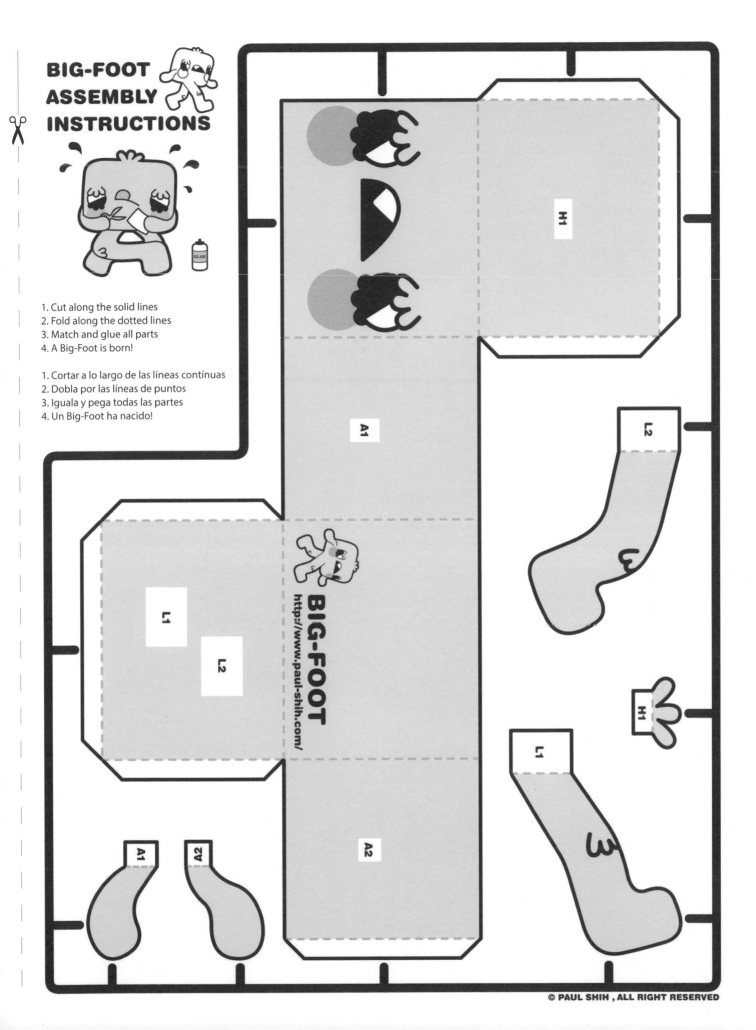

BIG-FOOT ASSEMBLY INSTRUCTIONS

1. Cut along the solid lines
2. Fold along the dotted lines
3. Match and glue all parts
4. A Big-Foot is born!

1. Cortar a lo largo de las líneas contínuas
2. Dobla por las líneas de puntos
3. Iguala y pega todas las partes
4. Un Big-Foot ha nacido!

GLUE

H1

A1

L1

L2

L2

BIG-FOOT
http://www.paul-shih.com/

H1

A2

L1

A1

A2

PAPER TOTEM!

HOLLOW THREAT
WWW.HOLLOWTHREAT.COM

HOLLOW THREAT

PAUL SHIH X PAPER TOTEM!

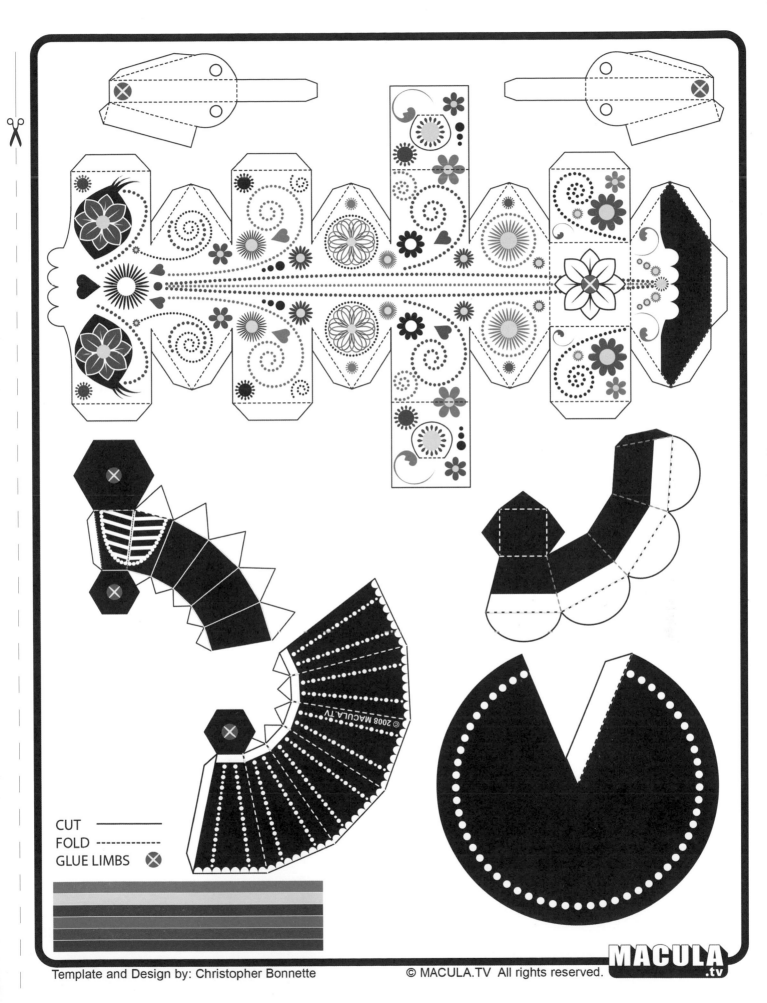

CUT —————
FOLD - - - - - -
GLUE LIMBS ⊗

MACULA.tv

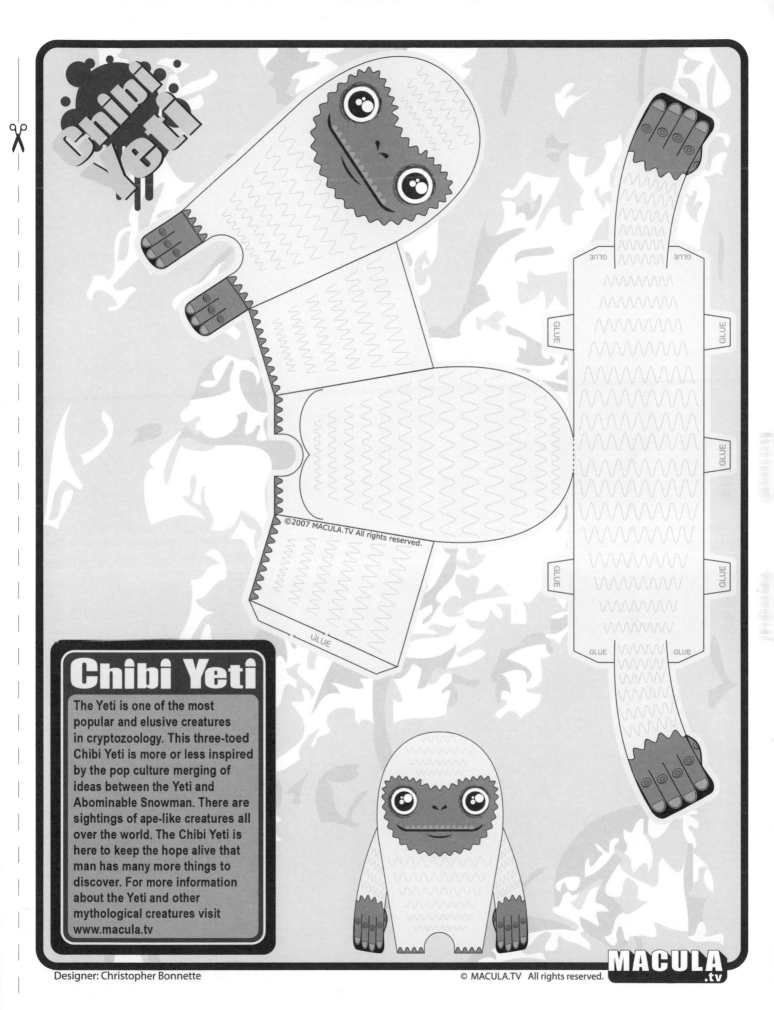

Chibi Yeti

The Yeti is one of the most popular and elusive creatures in cryptozoology. This three-toed Chibi Yeti is more or less inspired by the pop culture merging of ideas between the Yeti and Abominable Snowman. There are sightings of ape-like creatures all over the world. The Chibi Yeti is here to keep the hope alive that man has many more things to discover. For more information about the Yeti and other mythological creatures visit www.macula.tv

Designer: Christopher Bonnette

MACULA .tv

MUMMY

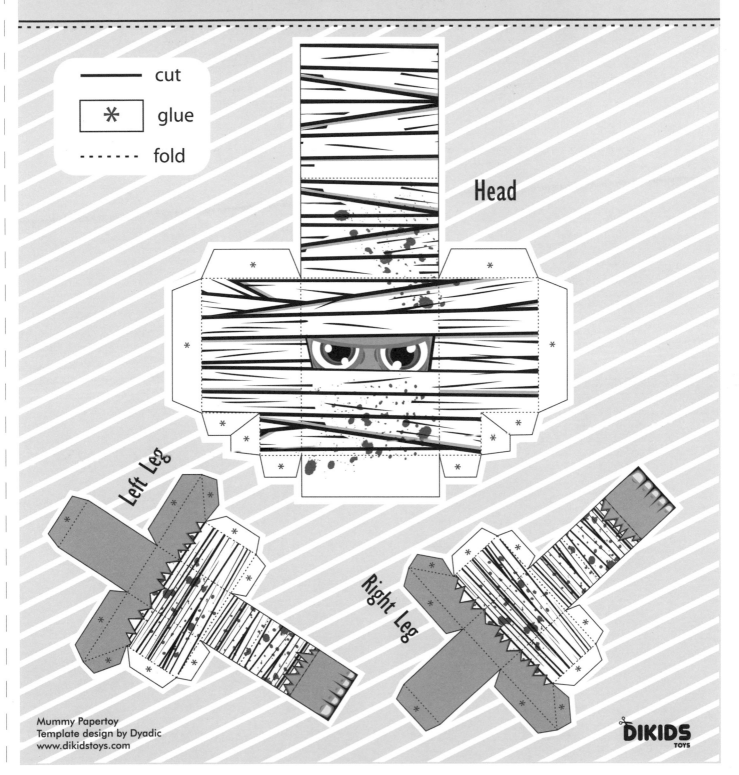

cut

* glue

fold

Head

Left Leg

Right Leg

Mummy Papertoy
Template design by Dyadic
www.dikidstoys.com

DIKIDS
TOYS

MUMMY

PAPERTOY INSTRUCTION

cut	fold	glue
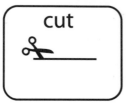	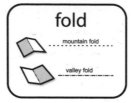 mountain fold / valley fold	glue 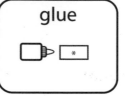 *

1. Cut out the template carefully using scissors or a craft knife by following the black lines.
2. Fold each part of the template (head, body, hand and leg)
3. Glue on the [*] using white glue or glue stick.
4. Attach all the parts with glue until turn into 3D shapes.
5. After all the parts is completed, unite all the parts (head, body, hand and leg) using white glue or glue stick.
6. Refer to the photo of the papertoy for help.
7. Always take your time when you build this papertoy.
8. Have fun and enjoy!

1. Recortar la plantilla cuidadosamente con unas tijeras siguiendo las líneas negras.
2. Doblar cada parte de la plantilla (la cabeza, el cuerpo, la mano y la pierna)
3. Extender pegamento en los espacios marcados con [*].
4. Unir todos los lados con pegamento hasta que se conviertan en formas 3D.
5. Una vez que las diferentes partes están completas, unir todas las partes (cabeza, cuerpo, manos y piernas) usando pegamento blanco o en barra.
6. Consultar la imagen del *papertoy* para obtener ayuda si fuera necesario.
7. Es importante no tener prisa montando tu *papertoy*.
8. ¡A disfrutar!

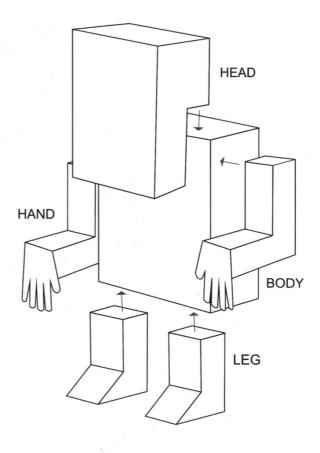

HEAD

HAND

BODY

LEG

www.dikidstoys.com

MUMMY

Body

Left Hand

Right Hand

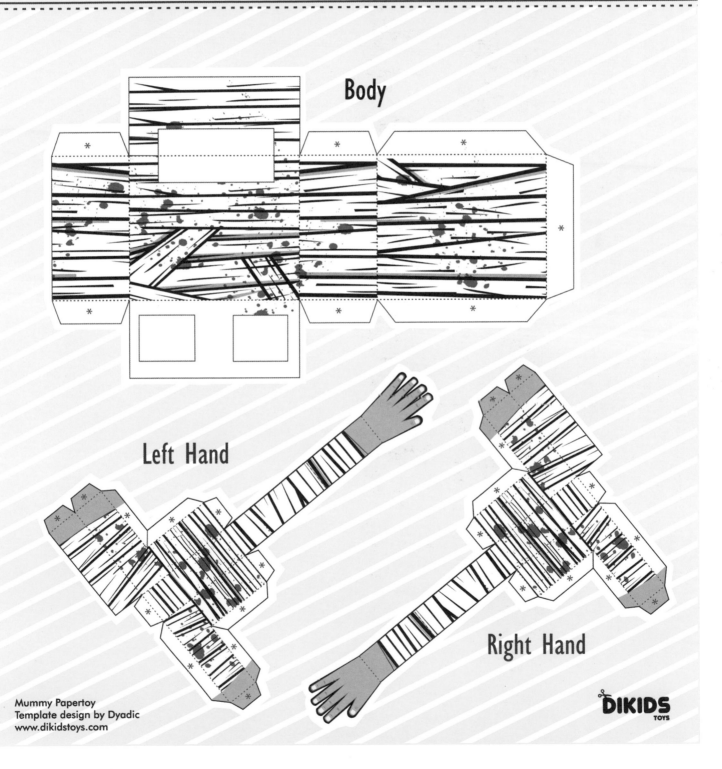

Mummy Papertoy
Template design by Dyadic
www.dikidstoys.com

DIKIDS TOYS

59

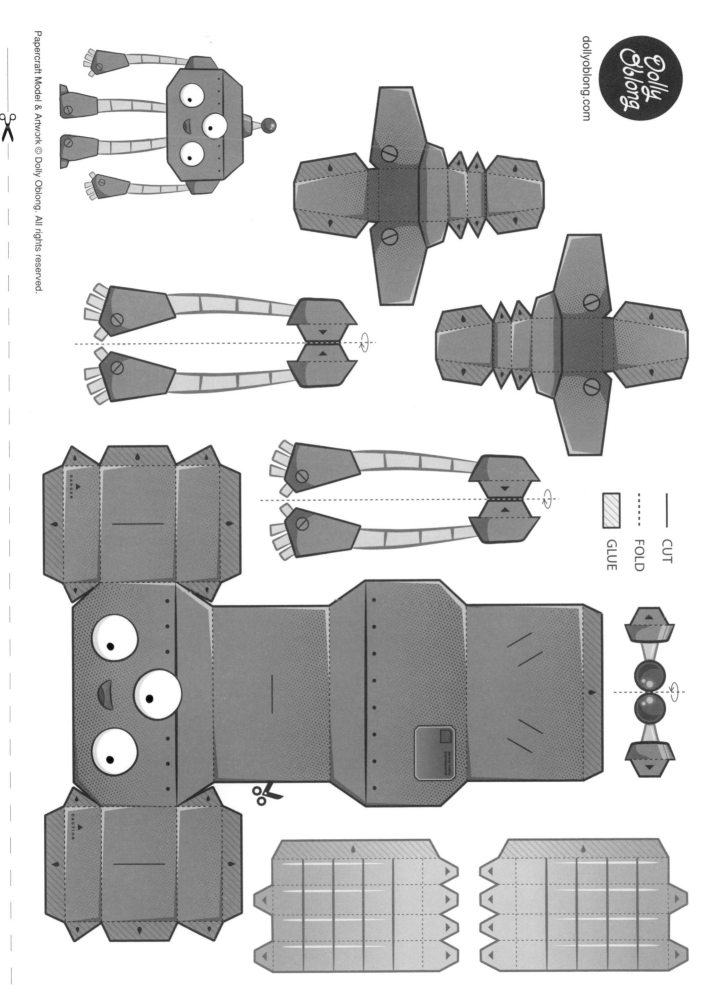

dollyoblong.com

Dolly Oblong

CUT
FOLD
GLUE

61

ZURG

Build your own PAPER TOY
Cut + Fold + Glue!

Dolly Oblong

dollyoblong.com

Dolly Oblong

——— CUT

······· FOLD

////// GLUE

GLUE
GLUE GLUE
GLUE
GLUE
GLUE

Horrorwood
CUTFOLD
STICKPLAY
WWW.HORRORWOOD.INFO

Y

GLUE
GLUE
GLUE
Y
GLUE

GLUE
GLUE
GLUE GLUE
GLUE
GLUE

X X

X

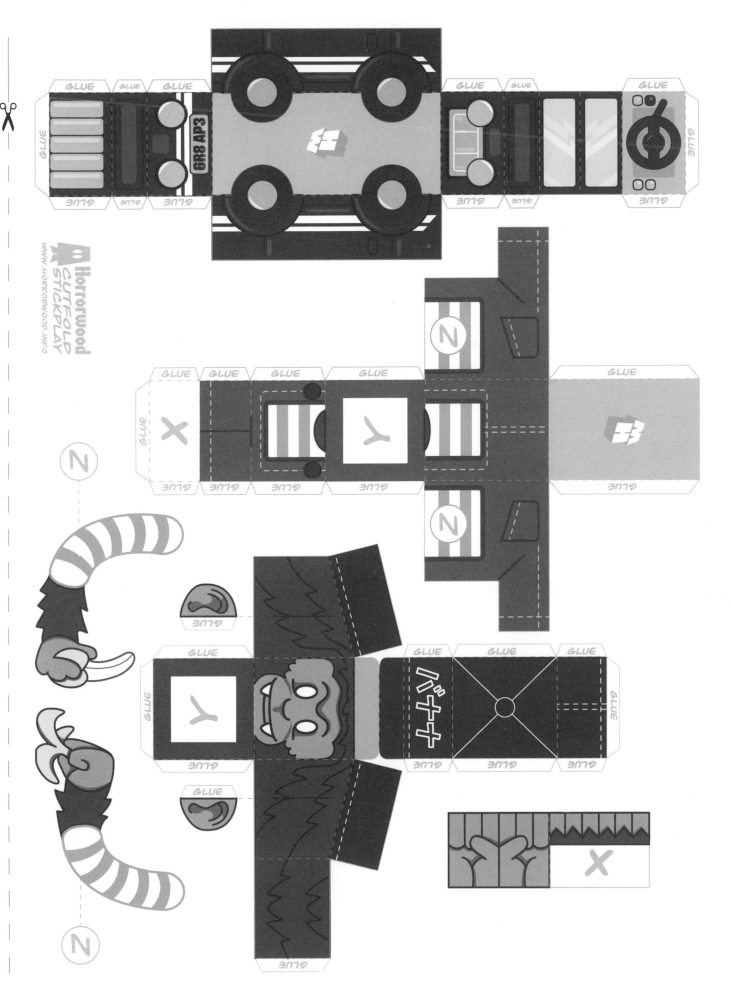

GR8 AP3

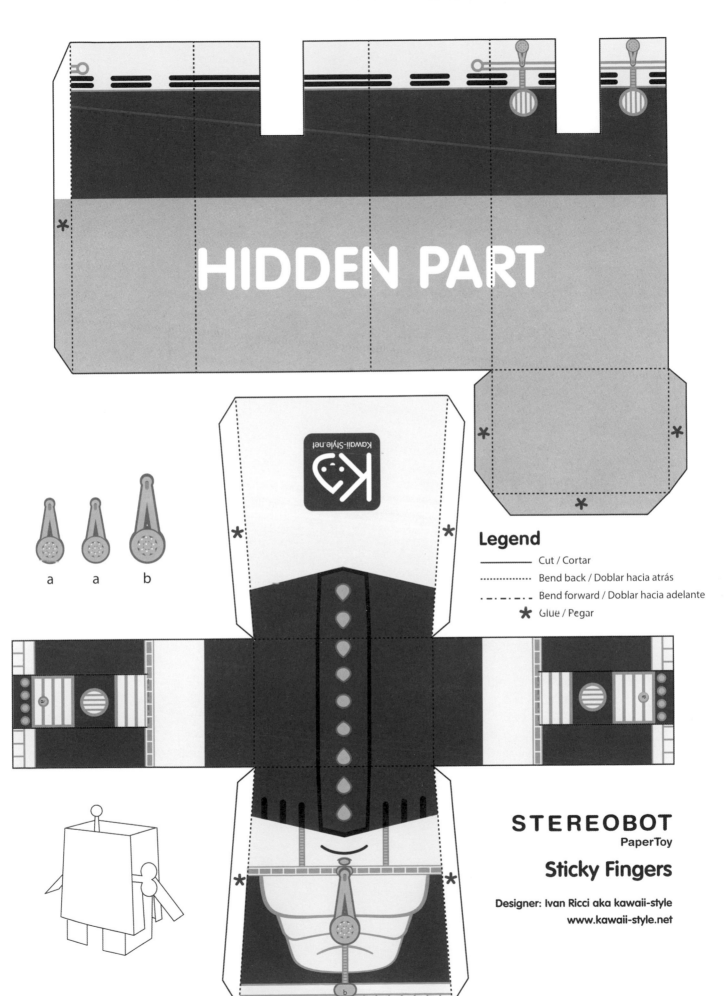

HIDDEN PART

kawaii-style.net

a a b

Legend

—————— Cut / Cortar

·············· Bend back / Doblar hacia atrás

—·—·—· Bend forward / Doblar hacia adelante

✱ Glue / Pegar

STEREOBOT
PaperToy

Sticky Fingers

Designer: Ivan Ricci aka kawaii-style

www.kawaii-style.net

Stereobot Sticky Fingers

ASSEMBLY INSTRUCTIONS:

1. Cut along the line.
2. Band back along the dotted line and bend forward along the dashed line.
3. Spread the glue in the spaces marked with an asterisk.
4. Paste the two sides indicated with the same letter. Insert the legs into the top body.

INSTRUCCIONES DE MONTAJE:

1. Recortar cuidadosamente.
2. Doblar hacia atrás por la linea de puntos, y doblar al revés por la linea discontinua.
3. Extender el pegamento en los espacios marcados con asterisco.
4. Pegar los dos lados indicados con la misma letra y encajar ambas partes.

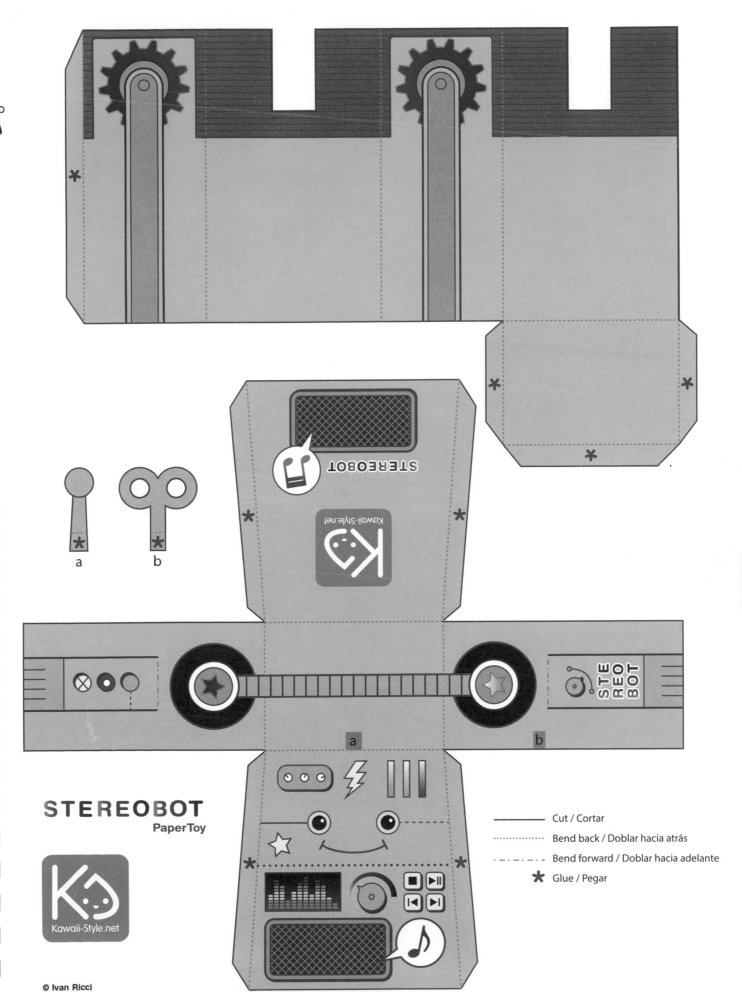

STEREOBOT

PaperToy

STEREOBOT

Kawaii-Style.net

STE REO BOT

a   b

——————— Cut / Cortar

················ Bend back / Doblar hacia atrás

– · – · – · – Bend forward / Doblar hacia adelante

★ Glue / Pegar

Kawaii-Style.net

Stereobot

ASSEMBLY INSTRUCTIONS:

1. Cut along the line.
2. Band back along the dotted line and bend forward along the dashed line.
3. Spread the glue in the spaces marked with an asterisk.
4. Paste the two sides indicated with the same letter.
5. Insert the legs into the top body.

INSTRUCCIONES DE MONTAJE:

1. Recortar cuidadosamente.
2. Doblar hacia atrás por la linea de puntos, y doblar al revés por la linea discontinua.
3. Extender el pegamento en los espacios marcados con asterisco.
4. Pegar los dos lados indicados con la misma letra y encajar ambas partes.

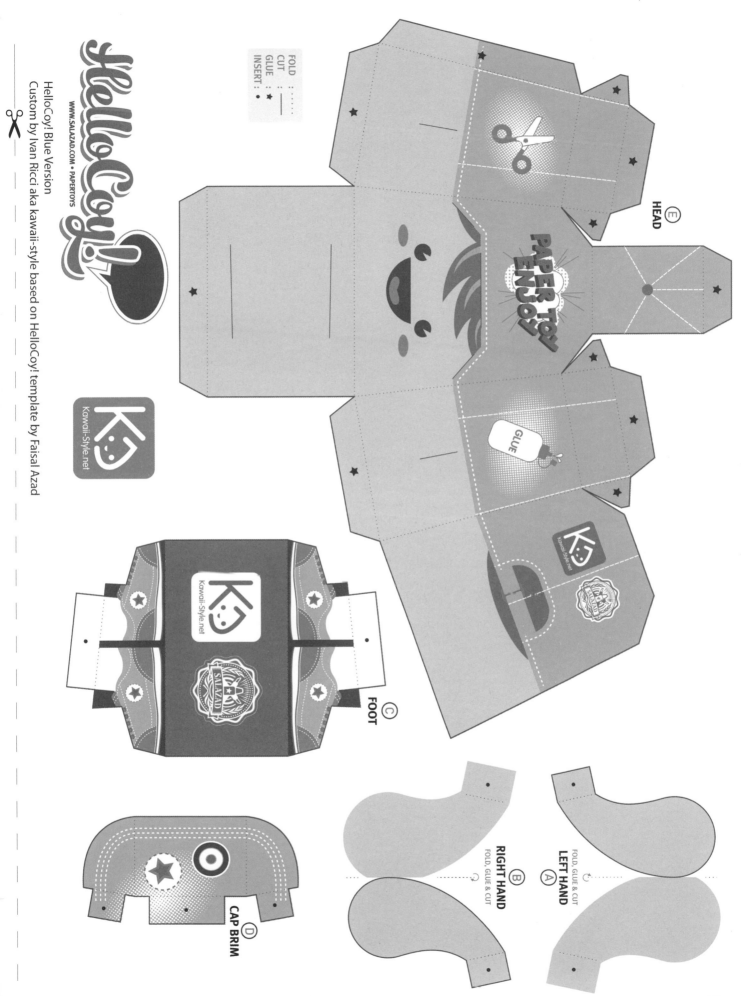

HelloCoy! Blue version

Design by Ivan Ricci, based on HelloCoy template by Salazad.

ASSEMBLY INSTRUCTIONS:

1. Cut along the line.
2. Band back along the dotted line.
3. Spread the glue in the spaces marked with a star.
4. Insert and paste the spaces marked with point.

INSTRUCCIONES DE MONTAJE:

1. Recortar cuidadosamente.
2. Doblar hacia atrás por la linea de puntos.
3. Extender el pegamento en los espacios marcados con una estrella.
4. Insertar y pegar los espacios marcados con un punto.

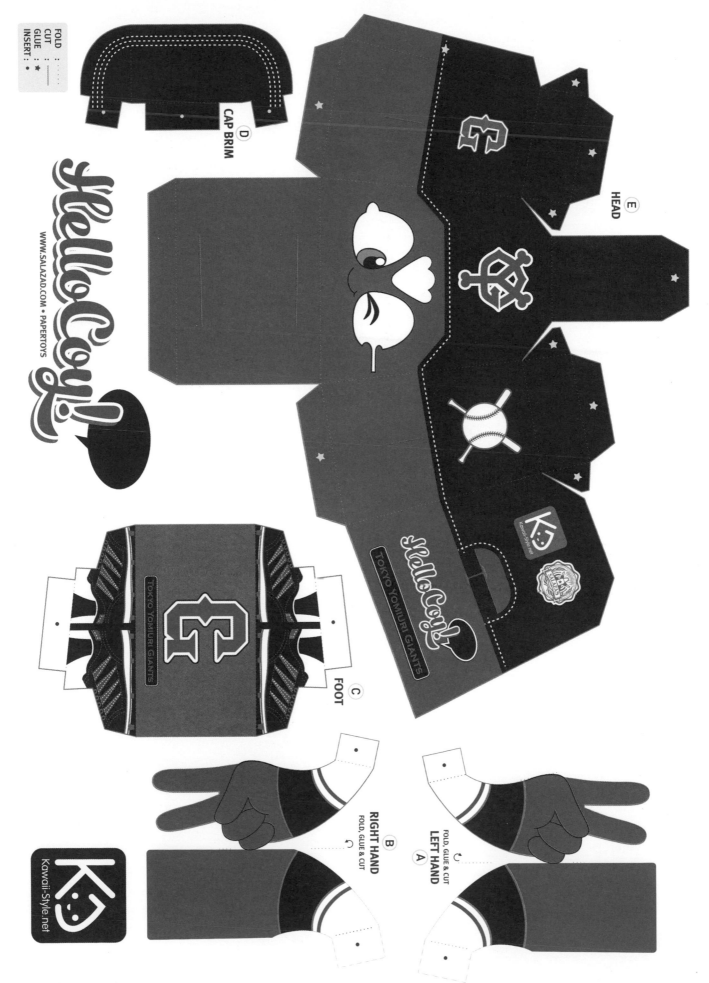

FOLD : ......
CUT : ——
GLUE : ★
INSERT : •

CAP BRIM D

HelloCoy!
WWW.SALAZAD.COM • PAPERTOYS

HEAD E

FOOT C

TOKYO YOMIURI GIANTS

HelloCoy!
TOKYO YOMIURI GIANTS

RIGHT HAND
FOLD, GLUE & CUT B

LEFT HAND
FOLD, GLUE & CUT A

KD
Kawaii-Style.net

75

HelloCoy! Tokyo Yomiuri
Design by Ivan Ricci, based on HelloCoy template by Salazad.

ASSEMBLY INSTRUCTIONS:

1. Cut along the line.
2. Band back along the dotted line.
3. Spread the glue in the spaces marked with a star.
4. Insert and paste the spaces marked with point.

INSTRUCCIONES DE MONTAJE:

1. Recortar cuidadosamente.
2. Doblar hacia atrás por la linea de puntos.
3. Extender el pegamento en los espacios marcados con una estrella.
4. Insertar y pegar los espacios marcados con un punto.

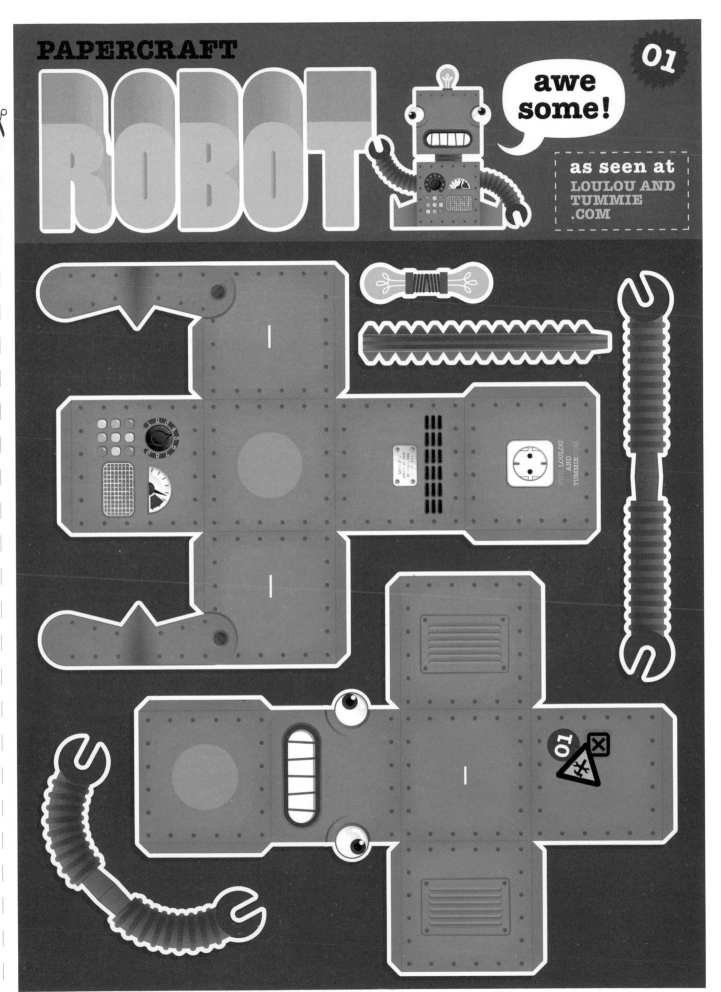

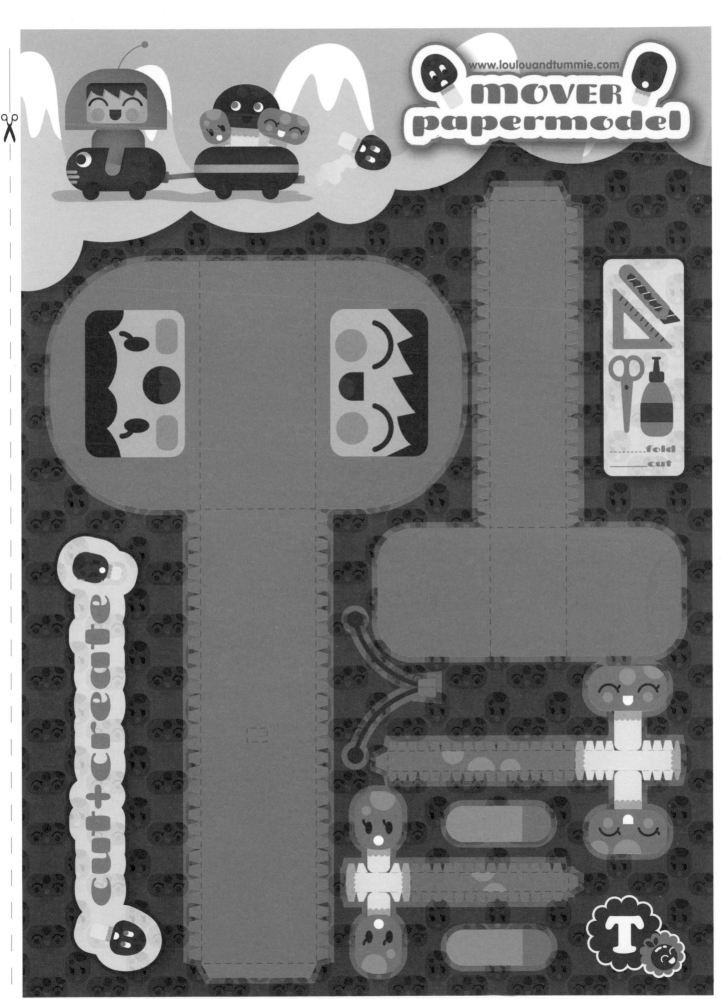

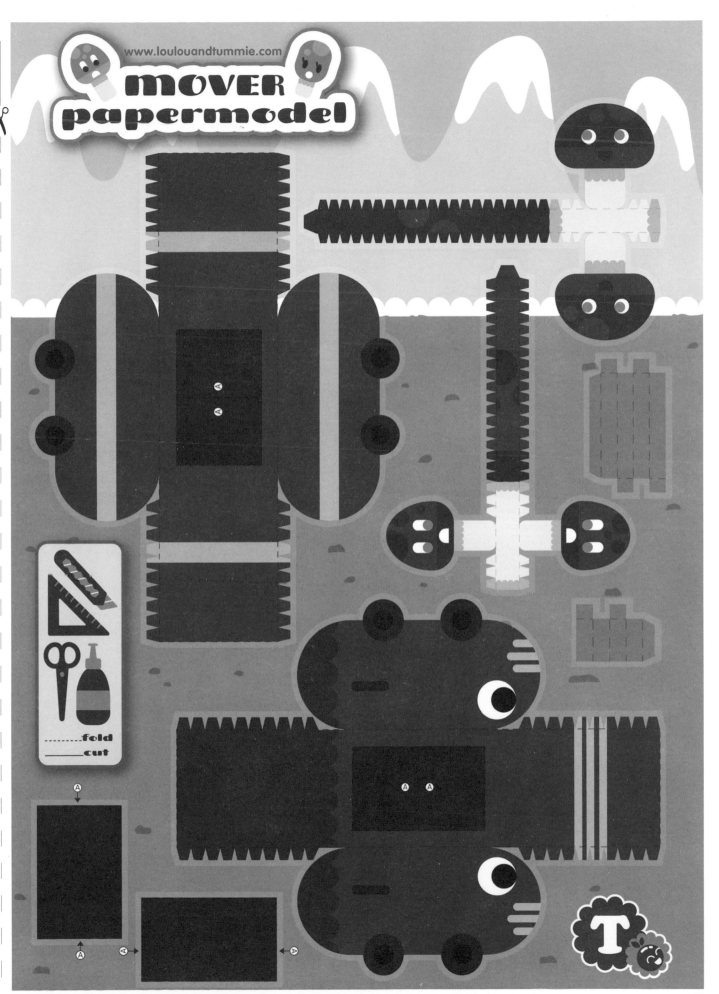

www.loulouandtummie.com

mover papermodel

..........fold
_____cut

81

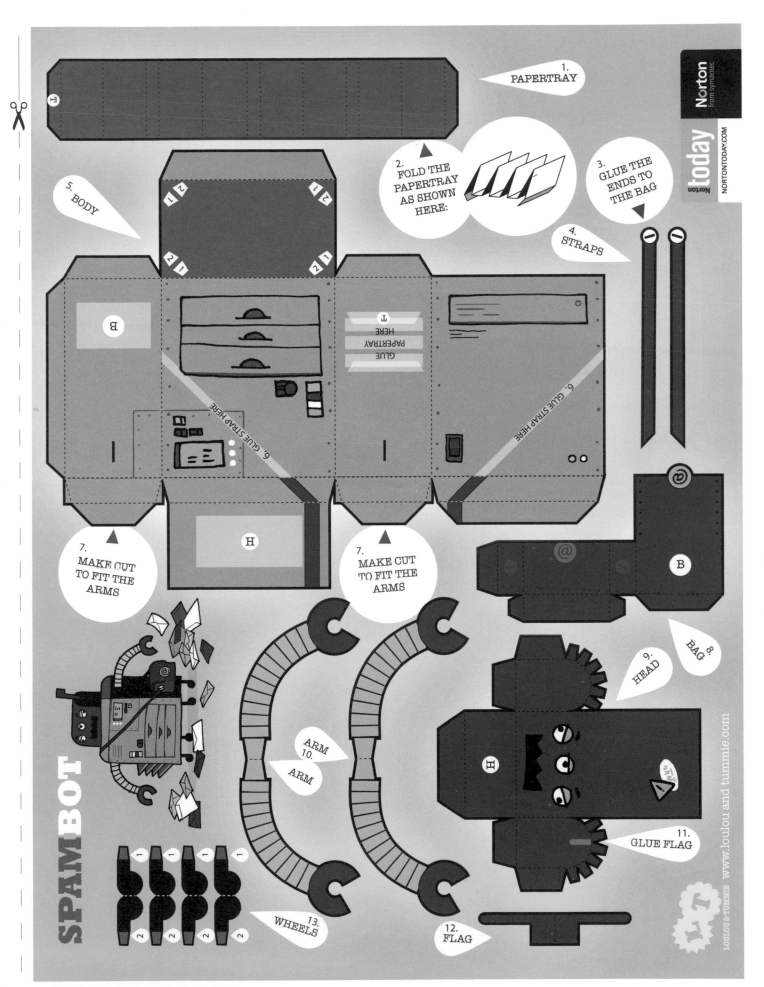

83

Spambot

ASSEMBLY INSTRUCTIONS:

1. Papertray
2. Fold the papertray as shown here:
3. Glue the ends to the bag
4. Straps
5. Body
6. Glue strap here
7. Make cut to fit the arms
8. Bag
9. Head
10. Arm
11. Glue flag
12. Flag
13. Wheels

INSTRUCCIONES DE MONTAJE:

1. Bandeja
2. Doblar la bandeja de papel como se muestra aquí:
3. Pegar los extremos al bolso
4. Correas
5. Cuerpo
6. Pegar las correas aquí
7. Cortar para adaptar los brazos
8. Bolso
9. Cabeza
10. Brazo
11. Indicación de pegamento
12. Marcador
13. Ruedas

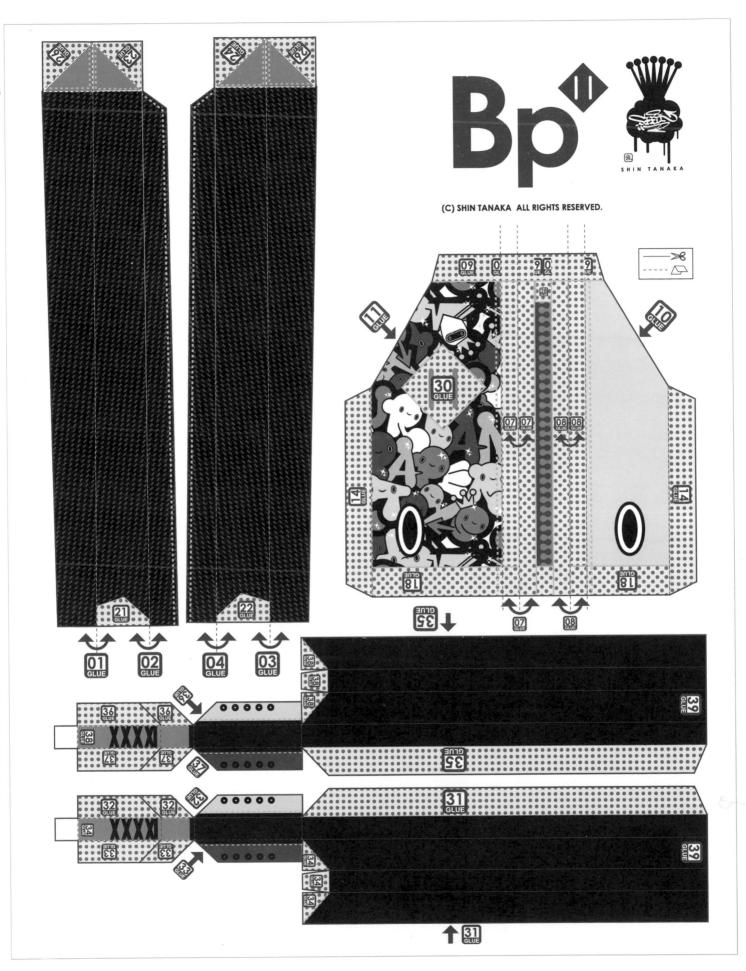

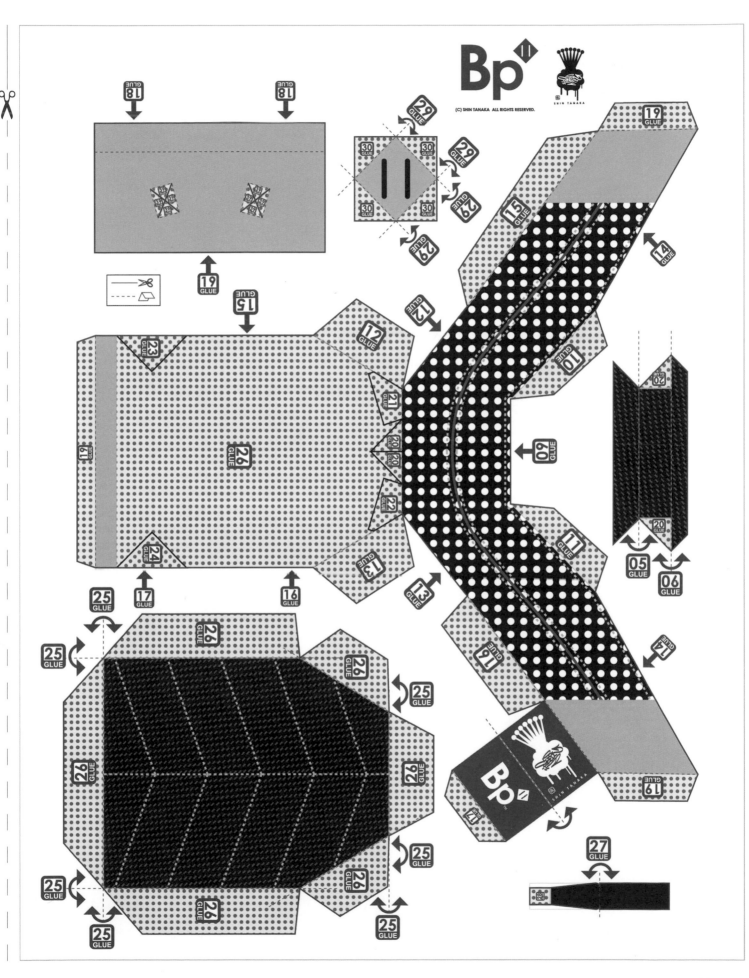

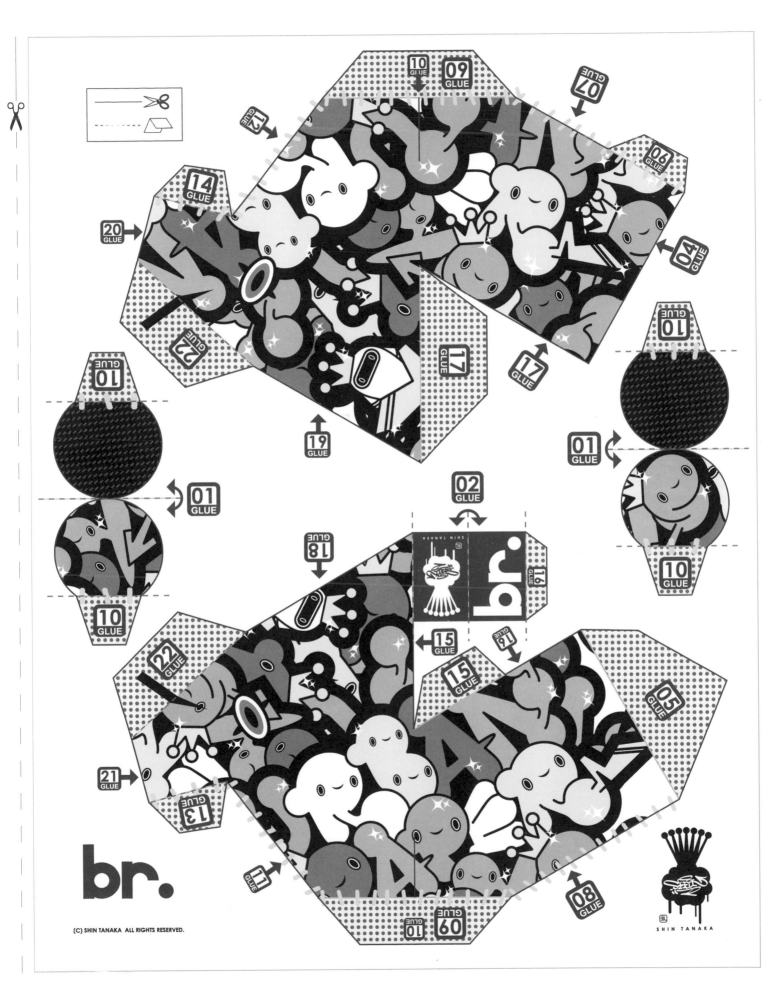

SHIN TANAKA

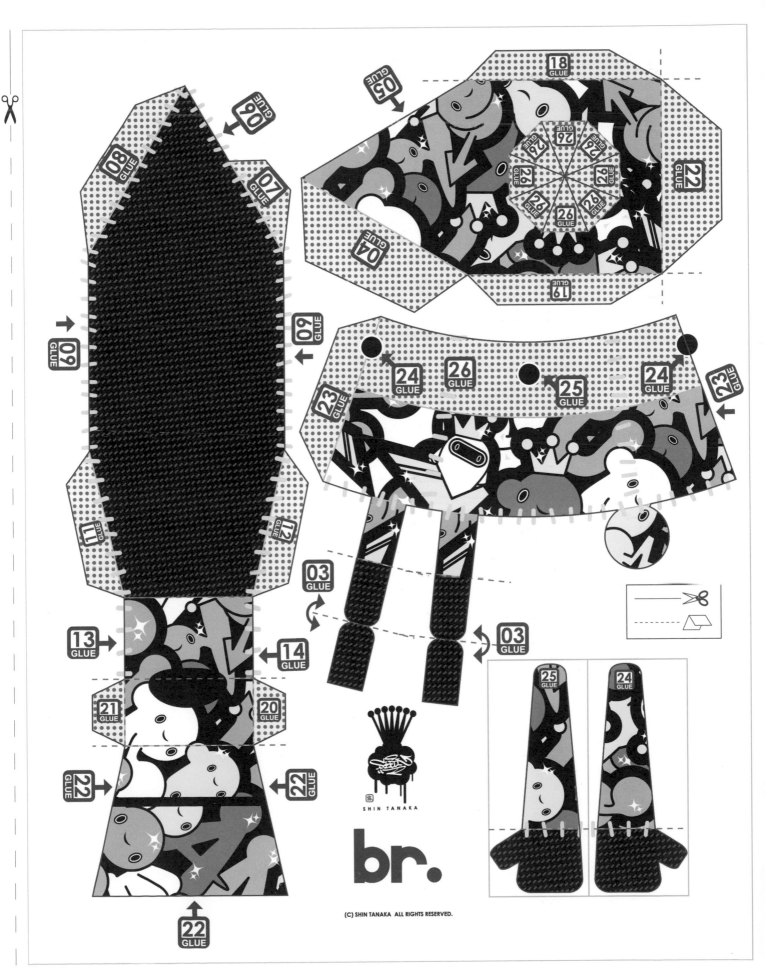

SHIN TANAKA

SHIN TANAKA

O.I.C.

SHIN TANAKA

(C) SHIN TANAKA ALL RIGHTS RESERVED.

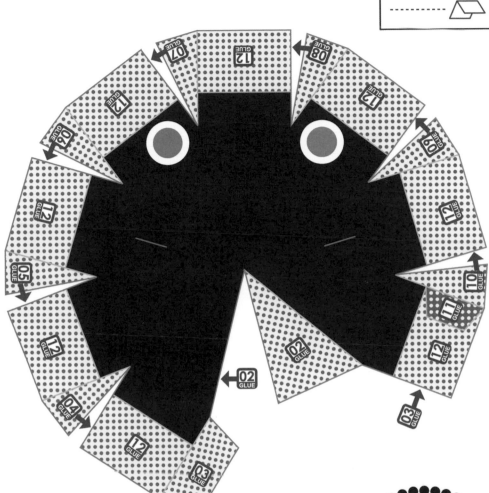

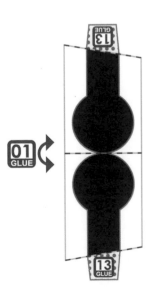

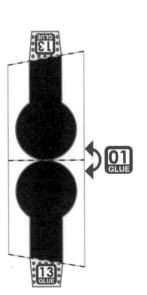

SHIN TANAKA

o.i.k.

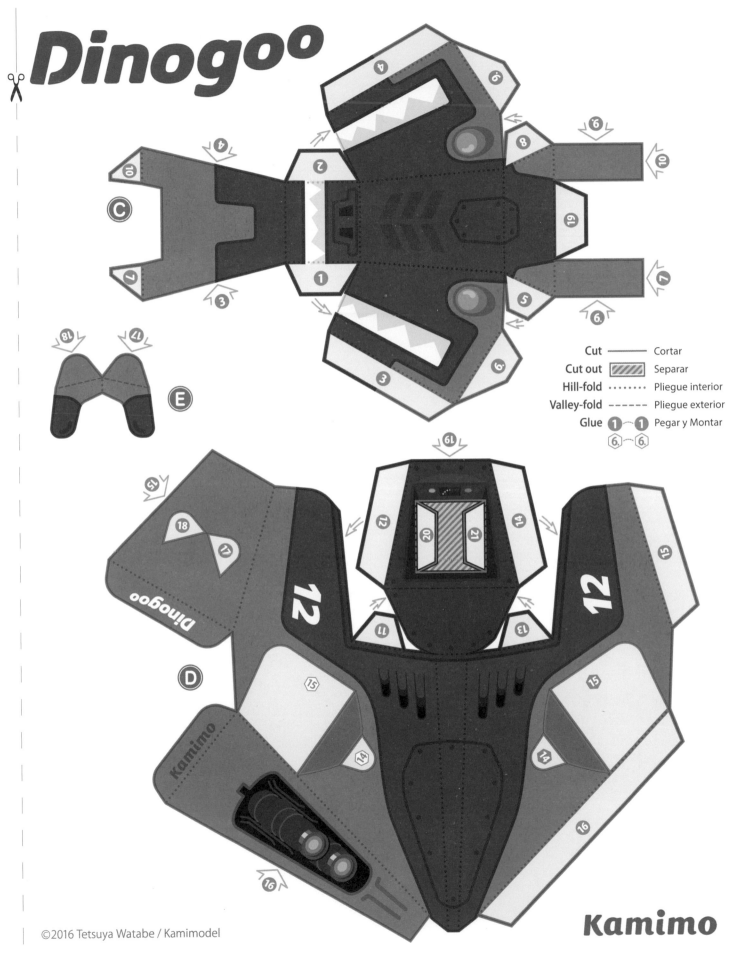

Dinogoo

Cut ——— Cortar
Cut out ▨▨▨ Separar
Hill-fold ········ Pliegue interior
Valley-fold ------ Pliegue exterior
Glue ①~~① Pegar y Montar
⑥~~⑥

Kamimo

Dinogoo

ASSEMBLY INSTRUCTIONS:

1. For folding parts, first use a dead ball point pen or other pointed tool to make a light crease along the fold line.
2. Cut carefully along the outer line with cutting blade or scissors.
3. Fold all these parts upward or downward as indicated.
4. Finally, assemble in order with the glue.

INSTRUCCIONES DE MONTAJE:

1. Para las partes plegables, utilizar primero un lápiz afilado u otra herramienta con punta para hacer un ligero pliegue a lo largo de las líneas.
2. Cortar Cuidadosamente por línea exterior.
3. Doblar las distintas partes hacia arriba o hacia abajo, como se indica.
4. Por último, unir las partes siguiendo el orden.

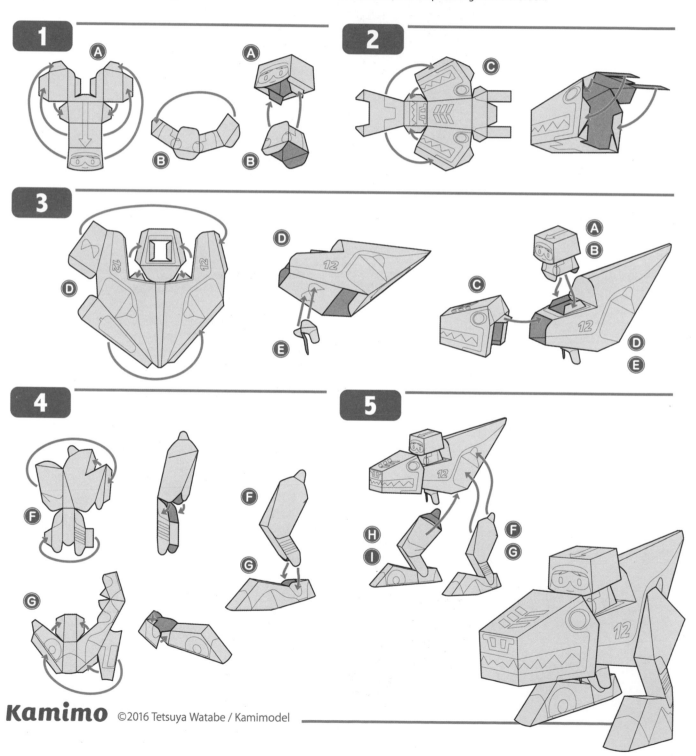

Kamimo ©2016 Tetsuya Watabe / Kamimodel

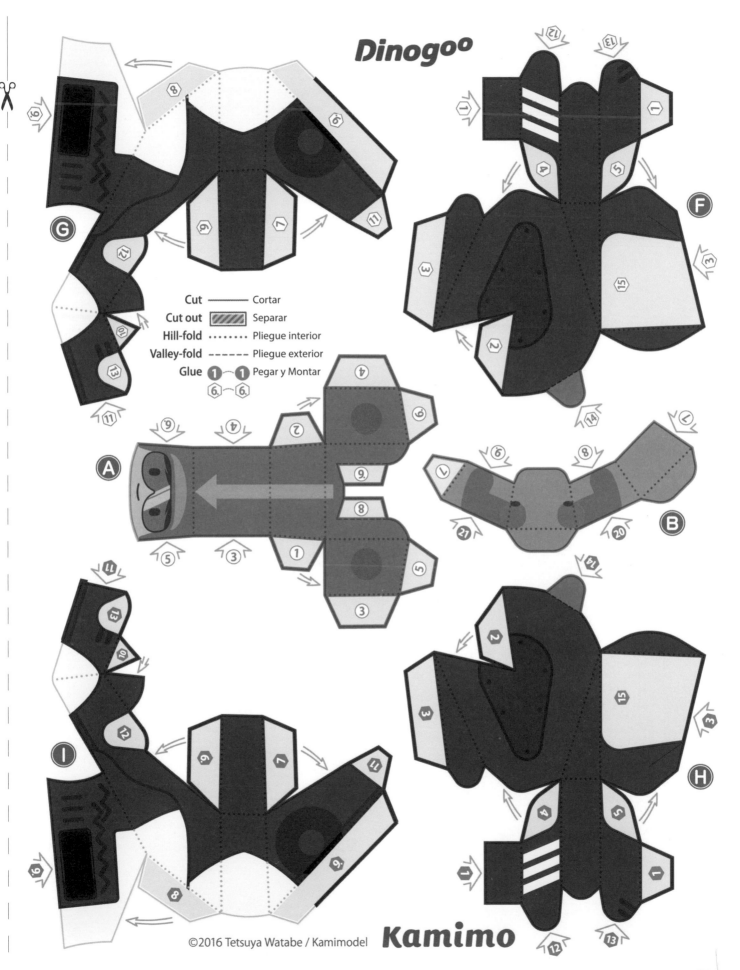

Dinogoo

Cut ——— Cortar
Cut out ▨▨▨ Separar
Hill-fold .... Pliegue interior
Valley-fold ------ Pliegue exterior
Glue ❶~❶ Pegar y Montar

Kamimo

Marky ©

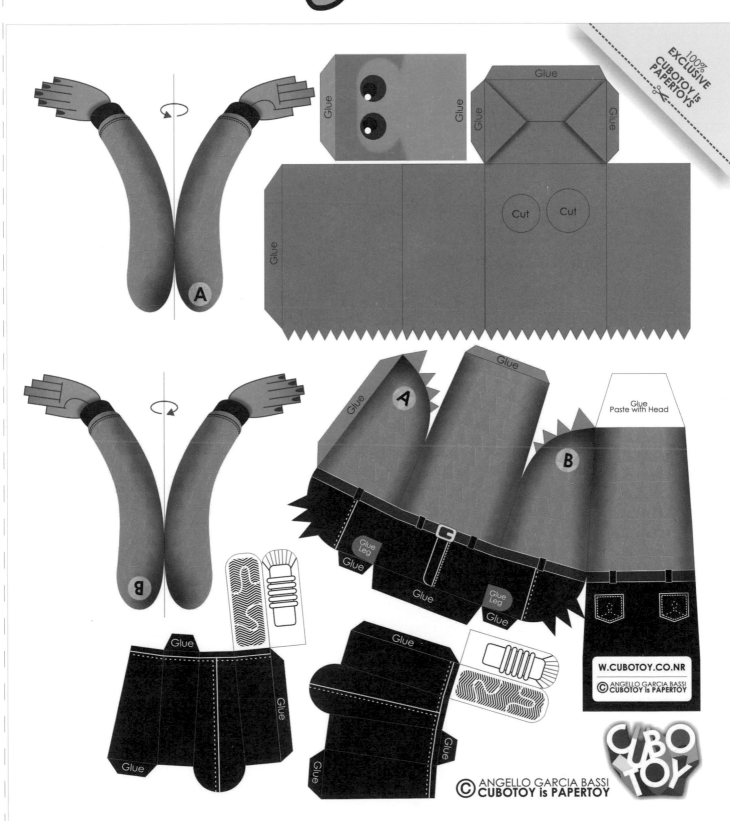

© ANGELLO GARCIA BASSI
CUBOTOY is PAPERTOY

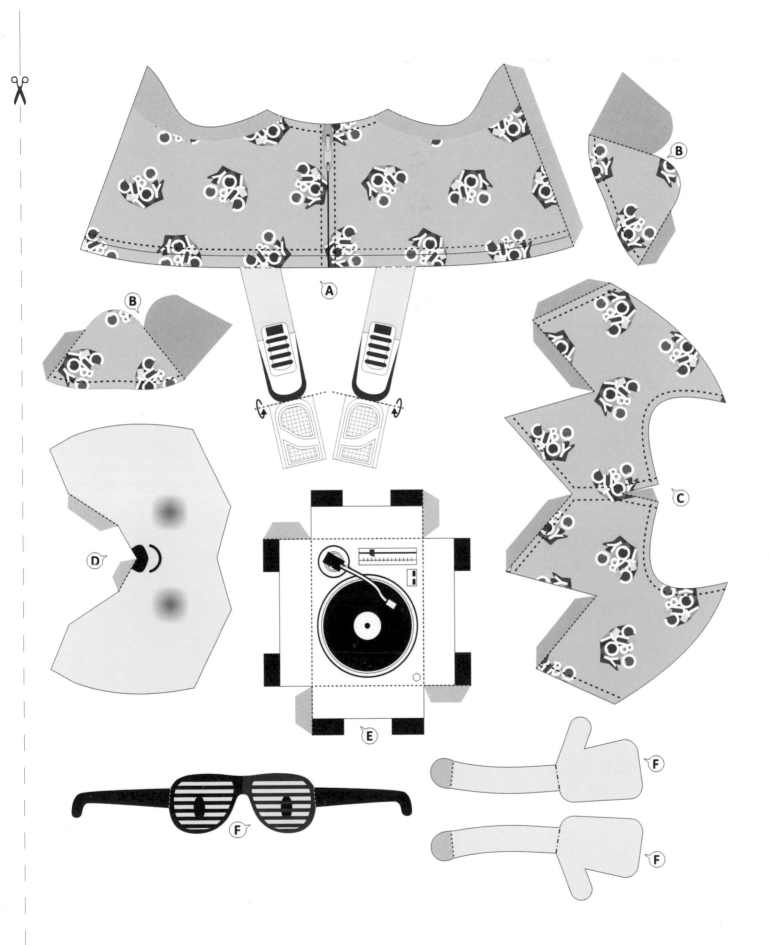

A

A1 - A2 Fold the legs and close the body using the tab at the back to form a kind of cylinder.
A1 - A2 Plegar las piernas y cerrar el cuerpo con la pestaña trasera para formar una especie de cilindro.

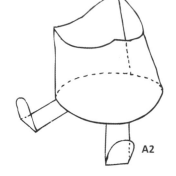

A1

A2

B

B1 - B2 Fold and paste the sleeves until they are completely closed.
B1 - B2 Plegar y pegar las mangas hasta cerrarlas por completo.

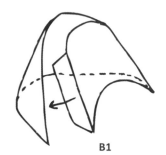
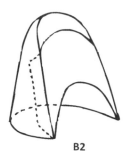

B1

B2

C

C1 - C2 Fold and paste the tabs to form the sweeter hoodie.
C1 - C2 Plegar y pegar las pestañas para formar el gorro del polerón (sudadera).

C3 Paste the sweeter hoodie following the lines indicated on the template and paste the sleeves to the sides.
C3 Pegar el gorro del polerón siguiendo las líneas indicadas en la plantilla y pegar las mangas en los costados.

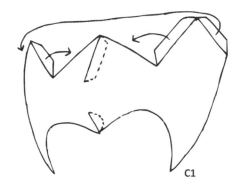
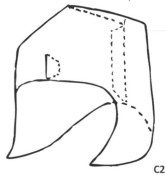

C1

C2

C3

D

D1 - D2 Fold and paste the tabs that form the character´s face.
D1 - D2 Plegar y pegar las pestañas que forman el rostro del personaje.

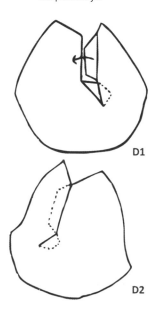

D1

D2

E

E1 - E2 Fold and paste the tabs that form the character´s record player.
E1 - E2 Plegar y pegar las pestañas que forman la tornamesa del personaje.

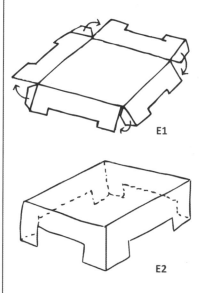

E1

E2

F

F1 Insert and paste the face inside the hoodie to accommodate the glasses. Then paste the arms to the inside of each sleeve.
F1 Insertar y pegar el rostro dentro del gorro y acomodar los anteojos. Luego pegar los brazos en el interior de cada manga.

F1

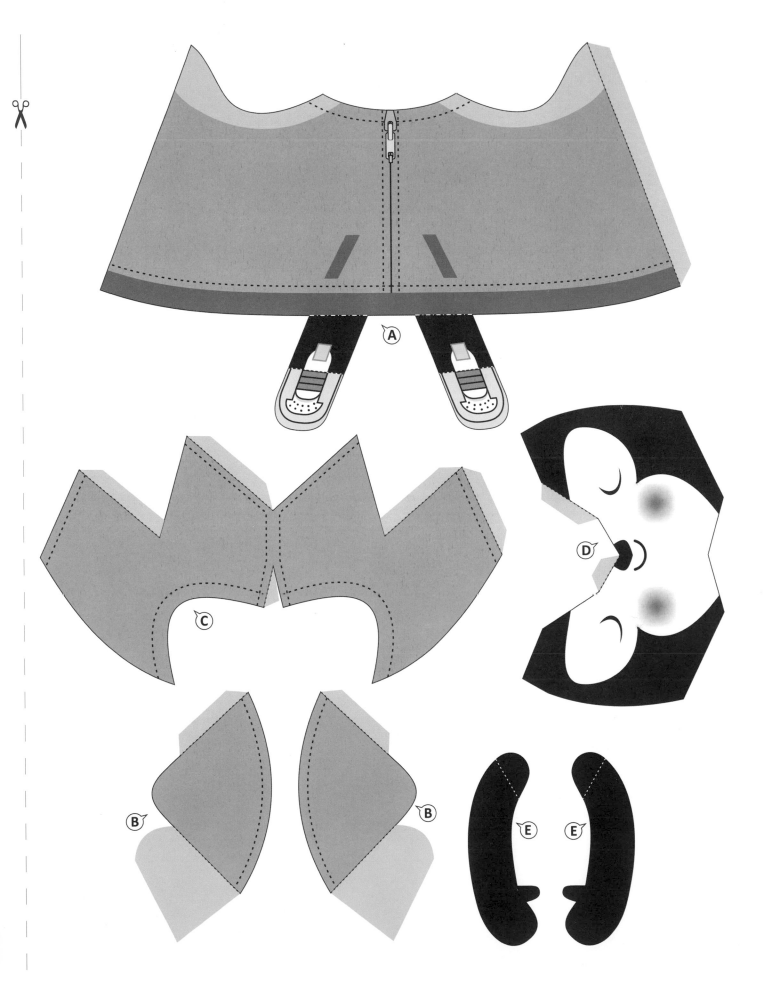

A

A1 - A2 Fold the legs and close the body using the tab at the back to form a kind of cylinder.

A1 - A2 Plegar las piernas y cerrar el cuerpo con la pestaña trasera para formar una especie de cilindro.

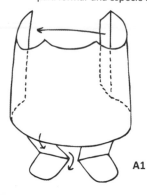

A1

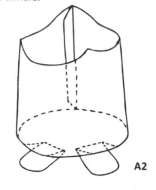

A2

B

B1 - B2 Fold and paste the sleeves until they are completely closed.

B1 - B2 Plegar y pegar las mangas hasta cerrarlas por completo.

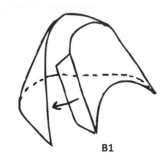

B1

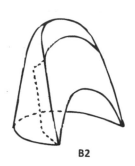

B2

C

C1 - C2 Fold and paste the tabs to form the sweeter hoodie.

C1 - C2 Plegar y pegar las pestañas para formar el gorro del polerón.

C3 Paste the sweeter hoodie to the lines marked on the template.

C3 Pegar el gorro del polerón en las líneas indicadas en la plantilla.

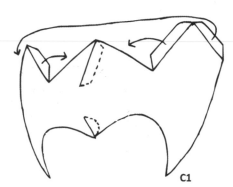

C1

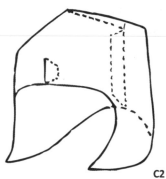

C2

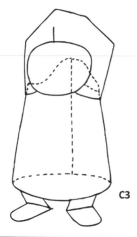

C3

D

D1 - D2 Fold and paste the tabs that form the character´s face.

D1 - D2 Plegar y pegar las pestañas que forman el rostro del personaje.

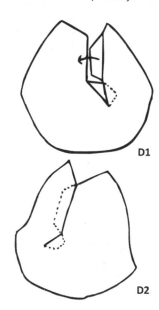

D1

D2

E

E1 Fold and paste the arms.

E1 Plegar y pegar los brazos.

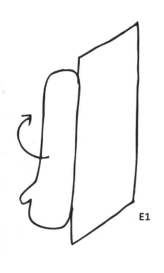

E1

F

F1 Insert and paste the face inside the hoodie and paste the arms to the inside of each sleeve.

F1 Insertar y pegar el rostro dentro del gorro y pegar los brazos en el interior de cada manga.

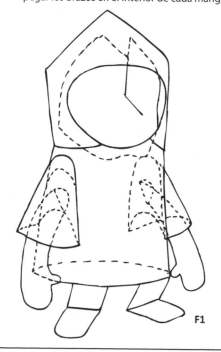

F1

A

A1 - A2 Fold the tabs as indicated on the diagram and then paste the tab to form the cylinder.
A1 - A2 Plegar las pestañas como indica el diagrama y luego pegar la pestaña para formar el cilindro.

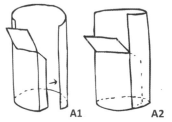

B

B1 - B2 - B3 Fold the tabs as indicated on the diagram and then paste the tab to form the cylinder.
B1 - B2 - B3 Plegar las pestañas como indica el diagrama y luego pegar la pestaña para formar el cilindro.

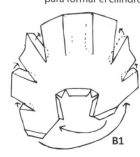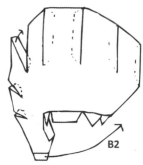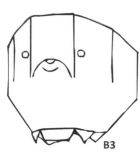

C

C1 - C2 Close the T-shirt using the tab at the back.
C1 - C2 Cerrar la polera (camiseta) por medio de la pestaña trasera.

C3 - C4 - C5 Join the head to the body using the tabs at the bottom of the head, pasting them to the inside of the T-shirt and breaking at the line closing at the back.
C3 - C4 - C5 Unir la cabeza al cuerpo por medio de las pestañas inferiores de la cabeza pegándolas por la parte interna de la polera y partiendo por la línea trasera que la cierra.

C6 Insert the cylinder inside the head and T-shirt, pasting the square of this structure inside the head.
C6 Insertar el cilindro por dentro de la cabeza y la polera, pegando el cuadrado de esta estructura por dentro de la cabeza.

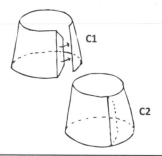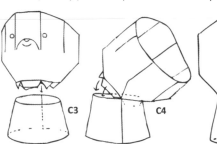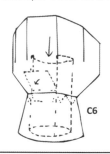

D

D1 - D2 - D3 Fold and join all the tabs until the body is completely closed by the arms.
D1 - D2 - D3 Plegar y unir todas las pestañas hasta cerrar por completo los brazos.

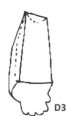

E

E1 - E2 - E3 Fold all the lines, respecting all the directions indicated by the dashed lines. Then paste the triangles that form the feet.
E1 - E2 - E3 Plegar todas las líneas respetando todos los sentidos indicados en las líneas segmentadas. Luego pegar los triángulos que forman los pies.

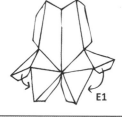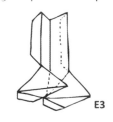

F

F1 Fold the tabs and the lines at the back side of the legs.
F1 Plegar las pestañas y las líneas de la parte trasera de las piernas.

F2 - F3 - F4 Join the front and back sides of the legs, fitting the shoes and pasting the tabs as indicated.
F2 - F3 - F4 Unir las partes delantera y trasera de las piernas, calzando y pegando las pestañas como se indica.

G

G1 - G2 Fold and join all the tabs to form the hair.
G1 - G2 Plegar y unir todas las pestañas para formar el cabello.

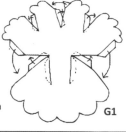

H

H1 Join the arms to the sides of the sweeter, fit the hair on the head, paste the glasses and insert the legs into the inner cylinder.
H1 Unir los brazos a los costados de la polera, calzar el cabello en la cabeza, pegar los anteojos e insertar las piernas al cilindro interno.